COMMUNICATING WITH EMPLOYEES

Improving Organizational Communication

Frank M. Corrado

A FIFTY-MINUTE™ SERIES BOOK

CRISP PUBLICATIONS, INC.
Menlo Park, California

COMMUNICATING WITH EMPLOYEES
Improving Organizational Communication

Frank M. Corrado

CREDITS:
Editor: **Andrea Reider**
Typesetting: **ExecuStaff**
Cover Design: **Carol Harris**
Artwork: **Ralph Mapson**

Distribution to the U.S. Trade:

National Book Network, Inc.
4720 Boston Way
Lanham, MD 20706
1-800-462-6420

Library of Congress Catalog Card Number 93-73208
Corrado, Frank M.
Communicating with Employees
ISBN 1-56052-255-0

This book is printed on recyclable paper with soy ink.

PREFACE

"What we have here is a failure to communicate."

—Paul Newman in *Cool Hand Luke*

In this wired global village that we inhabit today, there is more communication than we know what to do with. We are buried each day under a barrage of messages that exhort us to hear, see, smell, touch, feel, do, make and enjoy, but mostly buy. Billboards, television, radio, magazines, and maybe someday soon mylar ads in the sky are constantly sending out their steady stream of information.

For many of us the one refuge from this barrage of information and communication is our work setting. We can still go to work in the morning and find ourselves, unfortunately, in a sensory deprivation tank, where the only real information we get about anything is from the whispers on the grapevine.

In many companys' publications we get only bowling scores and birth announcements, but not last month's production numbers or sales figures. From supervisors we're lucky to get an annual, mandated performance review. Bulletin boards probably haven't been changed in months or years, and who has the time to look at corporate videos?

Surely, we don't want a brave new world where employees are subjected to a barrage of constant company *commercials.* There is too much work to be done. But in almost every organization, communications do need some real beefing up to stay even with this information age.

But no organization should ever think of communicating just for the sake of communicating. There is little room for that sort of altruism in today's incredibly competitive world. Communication of information in an organization makes sense only if it is a process that makes money and adds value.

That is what *Communicating with Employees* is all about. This book shows the way in which communication is an integral part of business, and helps you to use communication in a deliberate way to accomplish the business objectives of your organization.

Frank M. Corrado

Frank M. Corrado

ABOUT THIS BOOK

Communicating with Employees is not like most books. It has a unique ''self-study'' format that encourages a reader to become personally involved. Designed to be ''read with a pencil,'' the book offers an abundance of exercises, activities, assessments and cases that invite participation.

This book is for you to use in analyzing communication in your organization, and then developing a plan that will help you achieve your business objectives.

Communicating with Employees can be used effectively in a number of ways. Here are some possibilities:

—**Individual Study.** Because the book is self-instructional, all that is needed is a quiet place, some time and a pencil. By completing the activities and exercises, a reader should not only receive valuable feedback, but also practical steps in creating a more productive work force.

—**Workshops and Seminars.** The book is ideal for reading prior to a workshop or seminar. With the basics in hand, the quality of participation will improve. More time can be spent in concept extensions and applications during the program. The book is also effective when a trainer distributes it at the beginning of a session and leads participants through the contents.

—**Remote Location Training.** Copies can be sent to those not able to attend ''home office'' training sessions.

—**Informal Study Groups.** Thanks to the format, brevity and low cost, this book is ideal for ''brown-bag'' or other informal group sessions.

There are other possibilities that depend on the objectives, program or ideas of the user. One thing is certain: even after it has been read, this book will serve as excellent reference material that can be easily reviewed.

To Karen

With Great Affection

ABOUT THE AUTHOR

Frank M. Corrado is President of Communications for Management, Inc., International, a leading-edge management communication and consulting firm which has provided training and consulting to hundreds of profit, non-profit and governmental organizations throughout the United States and overseas. Mr. Corrado is also a speaker and travels extensively to address professional organizations.

Frank Corrado is the author of *Getting the Word Out,* published by Business One Irwin. For seven years he was on the faculty of Northwestern University's Kellogg Management School. He has also served as an organizational communications consultant with a number of national consulting firms on media, crises, environmental community relations, and organizational change. For more information on *Communications for Management* workshop programs, speaking availability, and assistance for your organization, contact:

Communications for Management, Inc., International
360 North Michigan Avenue, Suite 601
Chicago, Illinois 60601
1-800-875-0570

CONTENTS

INTRODUCTION

Try this quick audit of communication at your organization:

A. List *four ways* that your company uses to communicate with its employees:

____

____

____

____

B. List the *four real ways* that you find out what is going on:

____

____

____

____

Do the two lists match? Hopefully at least a couple of items are the same.

On the first list you might have jotted down:

- the company newsletter
- videos
- bulletin boards
- staff meetings

These may be the company's main communication channels. In many organizations, however, the *real way* employees find out what is going on might include:

- the grapevine
- conversations overheard in rest rooms or elevators
- a memo left on a desk
- the business section of a daily newspaper

If there is a difference between list A and list B, there is help ahead.

SECTION I

Conduct a Communication Audit

CHANGING COMMUNICATION NEEDS

"When in doubt, tell people too much."

—Robert Waterman, Jr.,
in *Renewal Factor*

Many organizations that have downsized layers of managers and workers are trying new approaches to boosting productivity, such as quality circles, self-directed work teams, and a renewed focus on mission, vision and values.

Management seems to be cutting back and, at the same time, giving more responsibility to employees. In this new environment, senior management knows it literally cannot afford to look at employees simply as a labor cost; rather they must see them as potential contributors to growth.

But today, the traditional employer-employee *contract* of longevity for loyalty . . . the guarantee of a job for life for a lifetime of dedicated and loyal service has evaporated as a result of cutbacks, downsizing and/or realignment. Companies are finding a cynical, uncommitted and discontented work force that is working longer hours and seeing more of its salary being put at risk in incentive programs.

Employee communication can help turn around this situation. It is the glue that can patch today's tattered working environment. The importance of communication in restoring a balance between the needs of the company and those of employees, and helping to restore and maintain credibility, is becoming apparent to more people. Strategic communication focused on accomplishing concrete business objectives is the order of the day as companies go back to the drawing board to reengineer their businesses.

CHANGING COMMUNICATION NEEDS (continued)

Communication is vital to the rejuvenation of all organizations.

There is a bigger communication job for everybody in today's flattened, spread-out organization. It is no longer a job just for somebody at the main office; every supervisor, manager and executive has to get involved.

The manner in which messages are being communicated is also changing in this new high-tech age. Electronic communication is supplementing, even replacing, print while managers are being asked to increase one-on-one and other high-touch forms of interpersonal communication. Today, there can be computer messages (E-mail) or voice mail sent to each employee from the CEO, as well as informal unit meetings and videos. This is a far cry from the formal memos of yesterday.

The content of organizational communication is also changing. The old newsletter was filled with birth announcements, gold watch presentations and team scores. Today, that newsletter and other communication channels carry stories on production targets, customer complaints and competition.

Organizational communication is also reaching out to a new kind of employee, one who is more diverse and multicultural—and very media savvy. The old message of *one big happy family* doesn't work in this new, diverse workplace, where continuous layoffs and downsizings, strikes, management shifts, reorganizations and bad press have become a daily reality.

Employee communication is driven by contradictions: high-tech systems with a high-touch emphasis, a need for credible information amid constant change, and relaying unified messages to a diverse work force.

QUESTIONS THAT GO BUMP IN THE NIGHT:

1. Can we have a good corporate image if we don't have a good internal image among our own people?

2. If an employee is not informed and loyal, and as a result does not exercise good judgment, how much impact could this have on the economic mission?

3. Do we have the capability to give employees the wide range of information they need—all the way from safety to equal employment opportunity information?

4. Can we have a real quality program without better communication?

5. Aren't middle managers the real problem in communication?

Employees have very simple communication needs—they want to know:

- what the problems are
- how the company is going to deal with them
- what their role as an employee is
- how they can become empowered to assume more responsibility

Organizations are realizing that empowered employees must be informed employees. If employees don't understand business issues, they cannot add value.

MANAGERS: WHERE COMMUNICATION GRIDLOCKS

Why are managers reluctant to share information with employees?

Check ☑ which of these reasons reflect current thinking in your organization:

- ☐ Giving away information means giving away power.
- ☐ Somehow the competition will get ahold of the information.
- ☐ Giving out information takes time.
- ☐ Rules are very strict on what we can talk about.
- ☐ It is too hard to explain business issues to employees.
- ☐ We don't know any more than the employees do.
- ☐ Telling the truth will make top management look bad.

When employees can't get information from their supervisors, they use communication backchannels, the foremost of which is *The Grapevine.*

Case Study: "We heard it on the grapevine . . . ."

"They're closing the lunchroom after 1 p.m. starting next week."

"No way."

"It's true. I talked to a guy who heard the cashiers talking."

"I can't believe it . . . "

"They think they will save money by doing it . . . "

When supervisors don't communicate with their employees, the grapevine fills in the gaps. The grapevine gives us a real-live person who seems to know what's going on. But today's educated employees want more information. They want to know not just *what,* they also want to know *why* and *how.* They cannot get that kind of information from the grapevine. That's where managers can beat the grapevine.

My Organization's Grapevine

Write down three rumors that you've learned from the grapevine. Then note whether they turned out to be true or false, whether management ever tried to deal with them, and how successful their effort was.

Rumor #1:

____

____

____

It turned out to be: ☐ TRUE ☐ FALSE

Rumor #2:

____

____

____

It turned out to be: ☐ TRUE ☐ FALSE

Rumor #3:

____

____

____

It turned out to be: ☐ TRUE ☐ FALSE

How can we help managers out? By making sure they get:

- timely information
- communication materials from professional communicators
- rewarded by their managers for communicating.

In addition to these traditional barriers to communication, supervisors today face an entirely different communication environment than ever before.

THE CHANGING WORK FORCE

The work force of today is very different from that of even 10 years ago.

Communication activities must recognize and reflect these changes:

YESTERDAY	TODAY
Homogenous	Diverse/multicultural
Authoritarian	Shared responsibility
Stable	Dynamic
Security and loyalty to the company	Loyalty to self and profession

In the new workplace, workers are diverse and multicultural, and have different values. They have less job security, but management wants expanded employee participation in decision making. Employees who now often define their lives in terms of their work have higher expectations for their jobs. In this environment managers must now *lead* rather than *boss.* This requires even more communication.

The way we communicate at work is also changing.

THE NEW WORKPLACE AND COMMUNICATION

The changing profile of workers is reflected in how they relate to communications techniques:

OLDER WORK FORCE	NEW WORK FORCE
Readers	Viewers
Not computer literate	Keyboarders
Formal communications	Informal
Ideas	Images as ideas
Focused attention	Short attention span
What was said	Who said it

To reach the new worker, new information communication technologies are being introduced.

Traditional Communication Technologies:

- Memos to employees
- Newsletters
- Formal supervisor/employee meetings
- Bulletin boards
- Company magazines

New Communication Technologies:

- Computer messages, E-mail
- Voice memos
- Videos/video newsletters
- Weekly tip sheets
- Interactive computer programs

GOOD ORGANIZATIONAL COMMUNICATION: A BIG PAYOFF

Good communication is good business. We've learned this from the Japanese who invest as heavily in their people as in their machinery. The idea is that the more people you have working on the problem, the better chance there is for success. Communication is the glue which bonds people working together toward a common goal.

The rush to install quality programs, empower employees to make decisions, solve problems at the lowest level, and reengineer the corporation will only be successful if it is based on a geometric increase in communication at all levels in the organization.

If employees are not given adequate information nor allowed to contribute to the solution of problems, they may revert to being the cause of them, resulting in increased absenteeism, lower productivity, grievances and so on.

The old rule of employee communication was "Tell them only what they need to know." The new rule is "when in doubt, tell them too much."

There are two parts to communication: a *systems* side that utilizes the right media, and a *human side* that delivers the information in a believable and empathetic manner. As one expert has said, communication must have body *and* soul.

Good communication is carefully planned from the top down, supported in writing, made part of a supervisor's performance evaluation, and focused on the business.

What are the characteristics of good communication? There are three major variables that we need to look at in evaluating organizational communication processes:

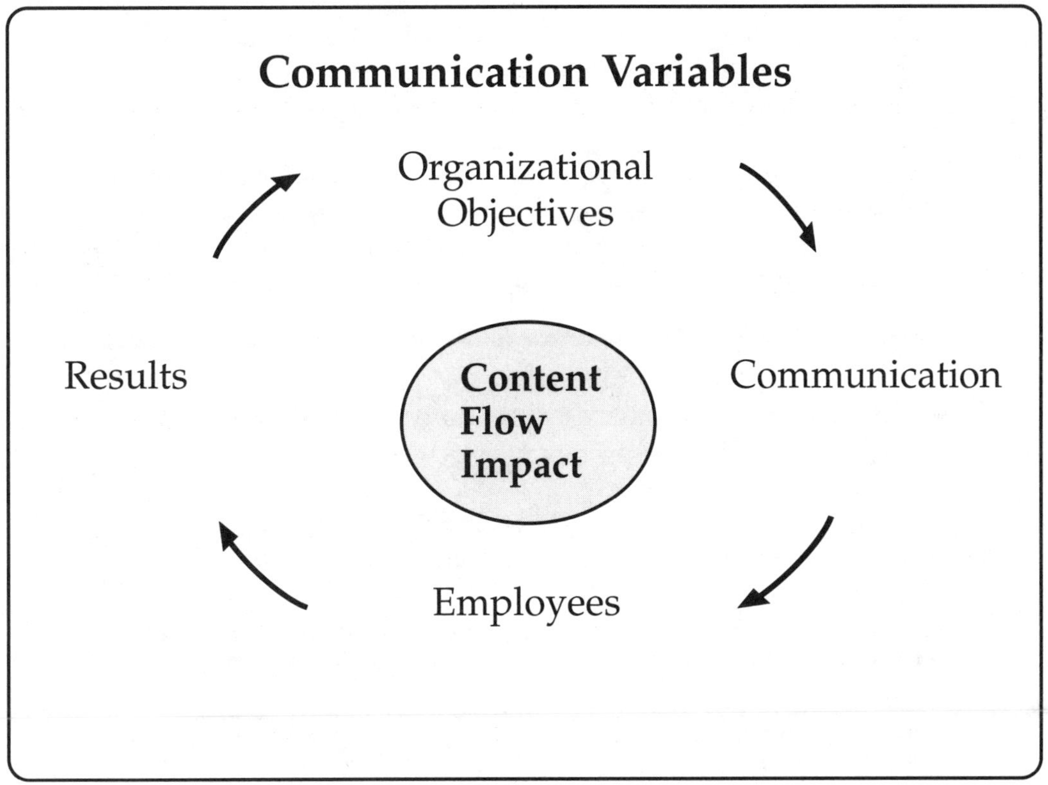

GOOD ORGANIZATIONAL COMMUNICATION: A BIG PAYOFF (continued)

1. **Flow:** how information moves through the organization to its audiences.

Mark each item T or F (True or False) as the following statements are applied to the flow of communication in your organization:

____ Feedback and suggestions flow directly to senior management.

____ Responsibilities for communication are defined and followed.

____ Supervisors understand the key issues and can answer employee questions.

____ Employees frequently receive information about other parts of the organization.

____ Grapevine information is closely aligned with formal messages.

2. **Content:** the type of information communicated and how it is targeted to specific audiences.

Again, mark each item T or F (True or False) as the following statements are applied to the content of communication in your organization:

____ Messages are targeted based on audience attitudes, information needs and media preferences.

____ There is a connection between current communication efforts and the economic mission of the organization.

____ Employees understand and support the goals of the organization.

____ Employees are aware of the issues and understand how they affect the organization.

____ Employees understand their benefits and utilize them wisely.

3. **Impact:** the results produced by communications efforts.

Also mark each of these items T or F (True or False) as the following statements are applied to the impact of communication in your organization:

____ Communication policies and practices are reviewed at least every three years.

____ Employee morale is excellent.

____ External audiences have a favorable view of the organization.

____ Communication efforts are evaluated 30–40 days after implementation.

____ Employees are committed to the goals of the organization.

Add up the number of ''Trues'' for each section. If you have fewer than three in any one section, you have flagged a problem area that needs to be addressed.

Communication is not one of the warm fuzzies of an original music track, with smiling worker faces on the video screen and sincere voice-overs—instead, it's the increase in units shipped this month, it's the uptick in customer satisfaction and the reduction in injuries. Great communication is like the telephone system; when it's really good, it's transparent—you don't even think about it.

THE NEW PROFESSIONAL COMMUNICATOR

Today's employee communicator has the job of providing managers and supervisors throughout the organization with the *messages* and *media* they need to get the word out.

The information that the employee communicator delivers can range from a revised benefits program to better management tips and to layoffs that will be announced to the press tomorrow.

Since communications must be more focused on creating value, a new type of communicator is emerging, one who:

- understands today's employees
- knows the mission of the organization
- understands the relative merits of new communication tools
- is responsible for making sure managers are trained to communicate and relay feedback information.

THAT WAS THEN	THIS IS NOW
Craftspeople	Strategists
Writers	Propagandists
Reporters	Storytellers
Primary communicators	Supporters of line communicators
Makers of things	Sellers of ideas
Always part of Public Relations	May be in Public Relations or Human Resources
Reactive	Preemptive

Today's professional employee communicator has more of a *strategic job*—developing communication strategies to achieve business objectives and then, with the support of top management, making sure supervisors and managers get the word out. This goes well past the old skills of just writing and producing materials.

There are three primary activities that any organizational communicator must be involved in:

- The first is *strategizing:* looking at a business issue and deciding how it should be communicated.
- The second is *toolmaking:* actually developing the communication materials based on the information that must be communicated.
- The third is the actual *delivering* or communicating of the messages.

Case Study: Applying New Communication Strategies

Dana Williams is in charge of employee communications for a company where senior management is beginning to understand the bottom-line implications of good communications. Before she joined the company, a new incentive pay program had been introduced during the last year for workers at the company's 18 manufacturing plants throughout the United States. The plan established a pot of money that plants can compete for, based on a complex formula. A four-color brochure was produced and shipped bulkmail to each facility, with a request that it be distributed to employees. Plant managers complained that the plan was difficult to understand, and many others just ignored it. In *strategizing* with the Vice President of Manufacturing, Dana realized that there *had* to be a communication system that would work at each plant. She decided that communications materials should be developed that could be used by the employee relations manager at each plant, and that the next time the plant managers came in for a meeting, both they and the employee relations managers would be trained to become experts in the subject matter. Moving to the *toolmaking* stage, she contracted for an overhead slide presentation to be developed, along with a simple two-color booklet that would more clearly explain the program. When the managers arrived for their meeting, half of the day was devoted to explaining the program and then providing the managers with slides, booklets and even a question-and-answer sheet so that they could be prepared for *delivering* the information and serving as interpreters for their plants.

THE NEW PROFESSIONAL COMMUNICATOR (continued)

Case Study Review Exercise

Write about an example using this new approach of *strategizing, toolmaking* and *delivery* in your organization. Some typical examples might be recycling, energy-saving, accident prevention, substance abuse or quality programs.

____

____

____

____

____

ANALYZING YOUR SITUATION

What is going on in your organization?

Is there constant confusion about what is happening?

Is the company going through restructuring without letting anybody in on the details?

Did anybody in the company announce how well it performed last month?

How well your unit performed last month?

Does anybody know what's going on around here?

How do you find out what is going on in your organization at any given time? Through the grapevine? The boss's secretary? How does information get to people; and how does information get back up the ladder?

There are a number of ways to find out. There are detailed communication audits that can be performed, and we'll talk about them shortly. But also there is a kind of *informal audit* that you can conduct yourself.

ANALYZING YOUR SITUATION (continued)

Exercise: Conduct an Evaluation

Using the approaches below, conduct an informal evaluation of communications in your organization:

Walkarounds

This is embarrassingly simple, but few people do it. In the management books they call it *management by wandering around.* You can not manage or communicate without good information. And some of the best information you're going to get on employee communication is going to come from walking around your own organization with your eyes and ears open.

This effort involves a lot of observation and note taking, but the information should be valuable. You'll get even better information by engaging employees in conversation, taking time to ask questions and listening to concerns about work and personal issues.

How do people address each other? ______________________________

____

What are the clues to status or job: dress, parking, eating areas? ________

____

How do people get together: in closed offices, in the hall? __________

____

What is on the bulletin boards? ________________________________

____

Does the suggestion box look used? ____________________________

____

Are there any motivators on the walls, such as signs or posters? ________

____

Do people seem busy and happy with their work? __________________

____

Lunchroom surveys

The employee lunchroom is as good a place as any to get an idea about employee communications. Are employees happy? Do they talk with each other?

Are informal discussions going on at the lunch table, or at the vending machine? ______________________________

____

What are people talking about? ______________________________

____

What are they worried about? ______________________________

____

What's the grapevine saying? ______________________________

____

Informal discussions

What are people's concerns when you get them together? ______________

____

How do people react when you bring up business topics? ______________

____

Is there some pattern to what people are saying? ______________

____

Are their stories about successes or failures? ______________

____

ANALYZING YOUR SITUATION (continued)

How do people view the company's future? ____________________

____

How do people see *their* future with the company? ____________________

____

Reading and viewing communications materials

Is the newsletter coming out on time? ____________________

____

What kind of stories is it telling: bowling scores or production reports? ____

____

What do the press clippings look like? ____________________

____

Is there a company magazine? What is it talking about? ____________________

____

Feedback channels

Are the notes in the suggestion box being read? ____________________

____

What's on the 800-line? ____________________

____

What is the sales/field force reporting? ____________________

____

You have just finished an informal communications audit.

Look over your answers and rank communications in your organization by circling one of the numbers on this scale:

1 = Major problems, lots of room for improvement

2 = Problems, but opportunity for improvement

3 = Good shape, but could use some fine-tuning

4 = No serious problems

Your Score ______

Now, with this information you should be able to get a good fix on the organization's communication *climate.* This will help give you the basis for *planning* an effective program.

S E C T I O N

II

Planning Successful Organizational Communication

DEVELOP YOUR COMMUNICATION PROGRAM

Once you have done an audit or survey, you have a fix on where the problems are. The next step is to develop a communication program.

There are three primary employee communication activities:

- Getting employees involved in meeting the organization's business objectives (the Seven-Step Employee Communication Program).
- Communicating basic information about the organization to employees.
- Developing human resource communication.

The Seven-Step Employee Communication Program

Step 1. RECRUIT A STEERING COMMITTEE

Step 2. ESTABLISH A COMMUNICATION POLICY

Step 3. IDENTIFY ACTIVITIES AND ASSIGN RESPONSIBILITIES

Step 4. BENCHMARK

Step 5. DEVELOP TARGETED PROGRAMS

Step 6. SET UP A BUDGET

Step 7. EVALUATE AND REVISE

DEVELOP YOUR COMMUNICATION PROGRAM (continued)

Step 1. Recruit a Steering Committee

An organizational communication program must start with the top management, which should put together a committee or task force. The group should include:

- top management
- human resources managers
- communication employees
- line management

A first step is to get this group to agree on some assumptions about communication.

Check ☑ which of the assumptions below reflect management thinking within your organization:

☐ "Employees who understand the goals and objectives of the organization, and their role in creating value for it, are more likely to support those goals and objectives."

☐ "Supportive employees who identify with the organization are less likely to leave or be absent."

☐ "Employees want timely information from their supervisors."

☐ "Managers will do a better job of communicating if you train them."

Step 2. Establish a Communication Policy

The organization now needs to articulate its beliefs about communication in a policy statement.

Check ☑ which of the following beliefs are generally held in your organization:

☐ Employees should understand the company's goals, the path toward achieving those goals and the employees' role in getting there.

☐ There should be open and continuous communication in all directions.

- [ ] Communication is a management responsibility, and managers' performance will be evaluated and rewarded based on how well they carry out these responsibilities.

- [ ] Employees are responsible for contributing ideas and suggestions to help their work units perform better.

- [ ] Information needs vary and the communication processes must provide the right information to the right people.

- [ ] A credible process can occur only when both good news and bad news are communicated.

- [ ] Employees should receive information at least concurrently with its public release.

The communication policy is the senior management's commitment, in writing, to employee communication. Key elements of that policy must include:

- A statement of mission
- The importance of communication in accomplishing the mission
- The policy toward communicating with employees

DEVELOPING YOUR COMMUNICATION PROGRAM (continued)

Here's an example:

> *"We can achieve our goals only if we have open, two-way communication at all levels of the organization. We recognize that we must keep employees informed about the business, as well as on issues of personal concern.*
>
> *We recognize that we have an obligation to give employees the information that they need to do their jobs. We also recognize that we will achieve maximum profitability only if we are open to the ideas and suggestions of people at all levels. As a result, part of every manager's performance evaluation will be based on communication effectiveness."*

Write out your organization's communication policy. If there isn't one, draft one:

____

____

____

____

____

____

____

____

____

____

____

____

____

____

____

Step 3. Identify Activities and Assign Responsibilities

We said above that there are three jobs in employee communication. The *strategy* job of developing the messages and tools for top management is usually given to a small staff at headquarters, but today, it can also be anywhere where managers are empowered to communicate. The job consists of deciding *what* must be communicated to *whom* and *how.*

The *toolmaking* (writing, photography, making videos) can also be done by the strategist, although the trend today is to outsource much of this activity. At the plant or store level there might not be money for this, so the budget will dictate how this will be accomplished. The *delivery,* or the actual communicating, is done in two ways: by *media* or by *manager.* Sometimes it is a combination of both.

Who is or should be responsible for communication strategy in your organization?

____

____

____

Who is or should be in charge of toolmaking?

____

____

____

Who is or should be delivering information to the lowest levels?

____

____

____

DEVELOP YOUR COMMUNICATION PROGRAM (continued)

Step 4. Benchmark

Benchmarking is a term often used in total quality management programs to fix performance at a specific point in time, so there are some standards to measure future actions against and to determine whether there has been any change. Looking at employee communication in our organization, we define benchmarking in much the same way. We need to measure, for example, employee support for a specific program. We need to find out where employees are on a scale ranging from *awareness* of the problem to actually being *committed* to taking action. We usually do this by conducting a survey among employees. This kind of research is much more specific than a general attitude or communication survey because the purpose is to benchmark against a specific objective that will create value.

Here is an example: If our benchmarking shows that the majority of employees of company X *understand* the company's program to reduce defects to three per one hundred thousand, but defects are currently at 20 per one hundred thousand, we know that we must develop a way to have employees take action that will cut these defects. We must set up a communication program that focuses on what action needs to be taken to reduce the defects, and then implement it. If the defects fall to three per hundred thousand, we know that our efforts have worked. If defects are reduced to 10 per one hundred thousand, we need to decide what our next step will be. Benchmarking gives real numbers with which to measure our communication success.

Once you have a good communication system in place, you can begin to concentrate on the really important task of producing creative value through letter communication.

Linking communication efforts to the goals of the organization is a foremost concern for communicators today. The key questions behind these concerns are:

- How does communication create value for the organization?
- How can this value be measured?

The need for this approach comes from today's organizational realities—companies exist to create value, and value is determined by economic performance in the marketplace. By increasing the amount of action taken by employees to achieve business objectives, an organization can improve its economic performance. The action can be expressed in many measurable ways, such as in reduced returns or customer complaints, faster turnaround, and increased productivity.

Some characteristics of this approach are that it:

- promotes understanding and commitment
- seeks feedback and participation
- provides motivation
- creates a basis for action
- monitors progress toward the accomplishment of organizational goals.

The role of communication is to move people toward action—having people do things that will help an organization to reach its business objectives.

Creating Value with Communication

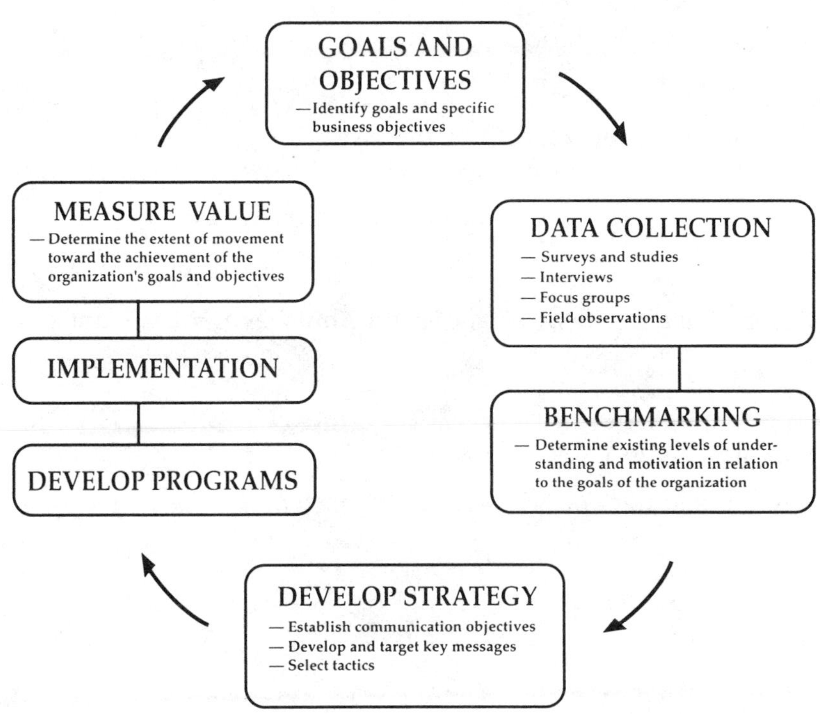

DEVELOP YOUR COMMUNICATION PROGRAM (continued)

Our objective is to be able to *measure some behavioral change,* or at a minimum, to measure movement along a scale that starts with awareness and ends up with action:

- **Aware**

  —employees have general awareness of the issue

- **Inform**

  —employees are up-to-date on issues involved

- **Understand**

  —employees have full understanding of the issues and implications

- **Accept**

  —employees accept the validity of the issue

- **Intent**

  —employees have decided to take action, but have not yet done so

- **Goal-Oriented Action**

  —employees take the specific actions requested

The question then becomes, ''How do we move employees from *knowing* about business objectives and understanding them to *taking goal-oriented action*?'' In the following continuum (developed at Communications for Management, Inc., International by Robert Nadeau), we see the various stages of commitment that employees pass through on their way to taking action:

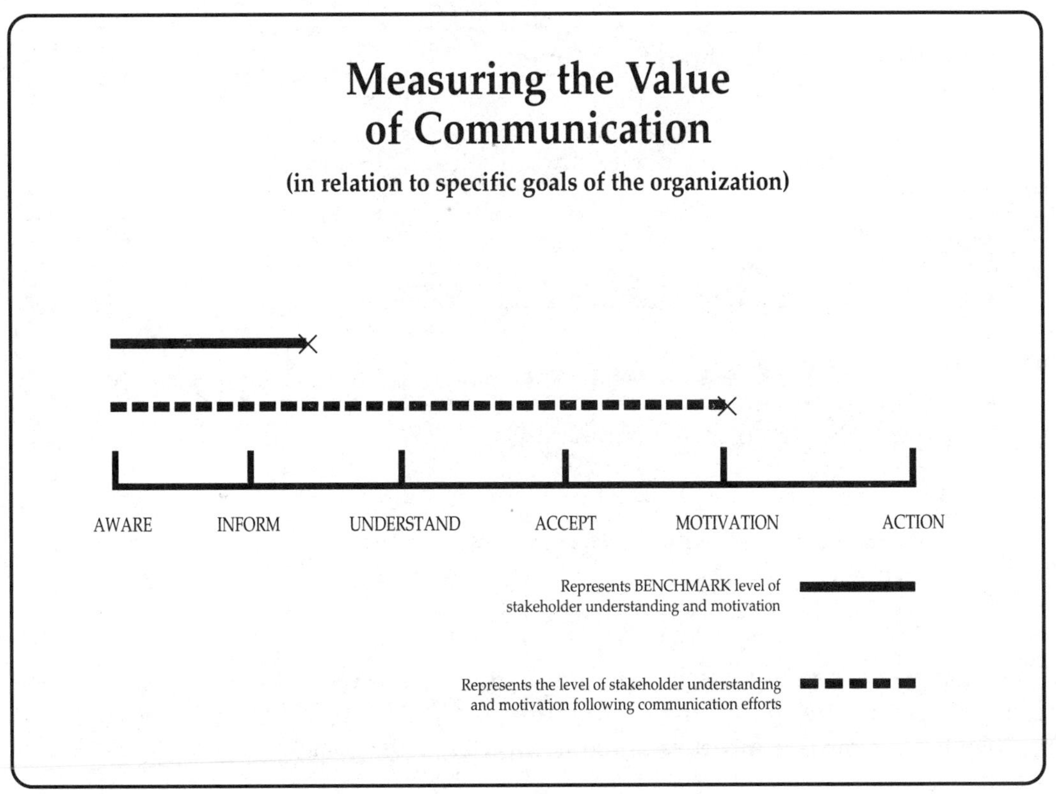

DEVELOP YOUR COMMUNICATION PROGRAM (continued)

This approach uses standard research techniques (See Section VII) to provide data which enables management to:

- establish a benchmark of existing conditions
- identify the information needs of employees in relation to the goals of the organization
- identify effective channels and media
- align communication policies and practices to the goals of the organization
- develop a long-range communication strategy
- identify forces and factors that could impede the successful accomplishment of organizational goals
- measure the relationship between communication efforts and economic performance.

This approach requires measuring employee commitment to specific business objectives, and then building a communications effort designed to move employees toward action that helps accomplish the goals and objectives of the organization.

In order to do this, we have to find out where employees are in terms of committing to, or buying into, organizational goals that can create value.

We must benchmark where employees are for each objective to help us see if the needle moves, and to identify the information needs of employee groups that will *motivate* them to take action. This benchmarking will also show us later how successful we have been in communicating.

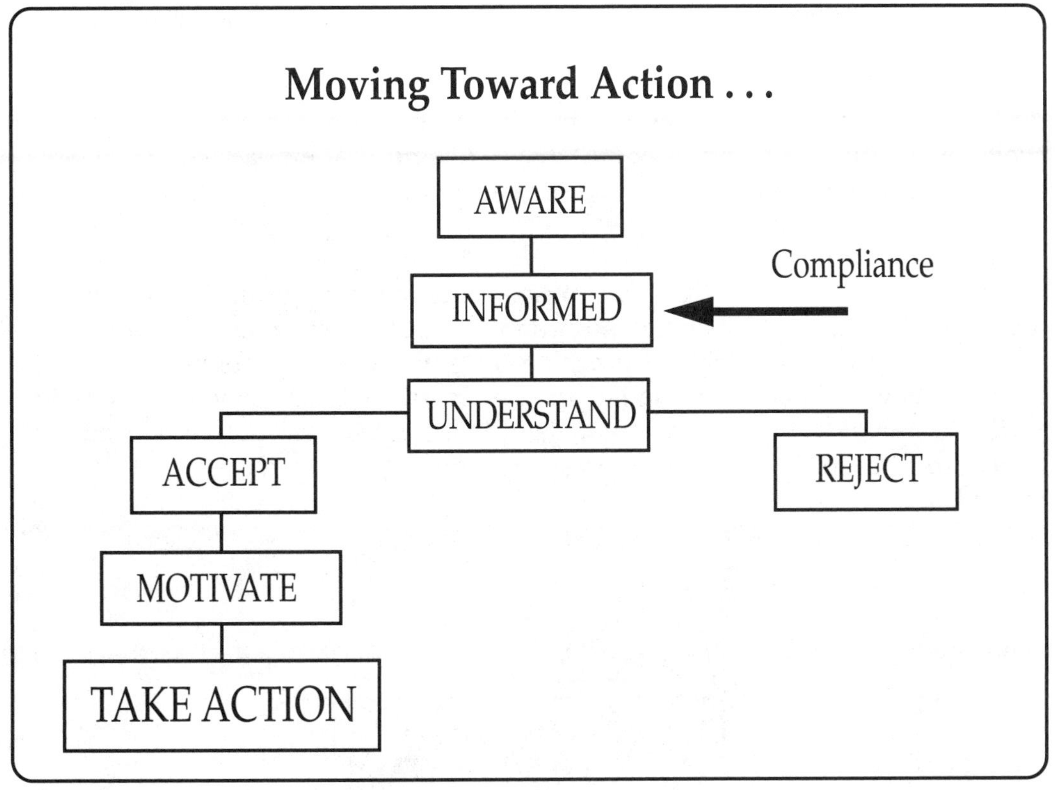

We should view each objective as a *marketing problem.* Employees are *consumers* of key organizational values or products: wellness, productivity, quality, customer service and safety. In establishing a communication program, research must be conducted first to determine the employees' level in terms of accepting each of the organization's goals.

Once we get employees to understand a need, we should assume that they will buy into it and will not reject it for reasons like management credibility, recognition or whatever.

COMMUNICATION BENCHMARKING

First, we have to establish *desired outcomes* that are linked to the organization's goals. For example, we might state that our objective is to *reduce product defects to two in one hundred thousand. Data collection* tells us that one hundred and twenty employees are involved in production, and none are on incentive programs. In the next step, *benchmarking,* we learn that employees are aware that the present defect rate is twelve in one hundred thousand, but do not consider this a serious problem.

After brainstorming, we *develop a strategy* of dividing the group into work teams and instituting an incentive program. We put together our communication *toolmaking* (or tactics), which includes a group meeting to announce the program as well as team briefings by supervisors. *Implementation* (or delivery) takes place over a three-week period, and *measurement* takes place two months afterward in order to observe progress and to establish corrections if they are needed.

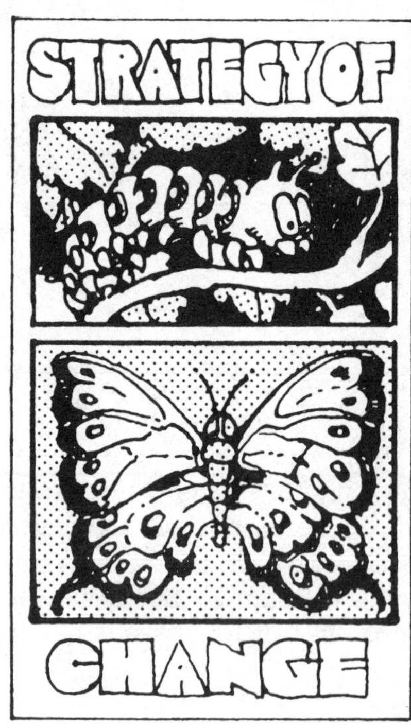

Exercise: Benchmarking

On the planning matrix provided, write out one business objective. Plot where you believe employees are on the scale, and what action plan you might take to move employees toward taking action.

Planning Matrix	
Organizational Goal:	Stakeholder Group:
Desired Action:	
Existing Conditions: (please indicate) Aware — Informed — Understands — Accepts — Motivated — Taking Action	
Action Plan:	

Step 5. Develop Targeted Programs

Moving the needle may take time. You may try one approach and see that it doesn't have much impact, so you may need to try another. If good evaluation and feedback loops are built into our efforts to move the needle, we will be successful. This is no different from what is done in any manufacturing organization—keep tinkering until you get it right. Our long-range goal will be to achieve higher profitability. Our short-range objective might be to cut grievances and lost time due to accidents, or to reduce scrap.

COMMUNICATION BENCHMARKING (continued)

Step 6. Set Up a Budget

"What does this all cost?" This is the familiar cry of skeptical accountants, number-crunching MBAs who influence senior management. This is also where communicators usually start mumbling about intangibles.

Costs will vary, but generally investments in employee communication are not very high. The greatest results usually come from improved supervisor-to-employee communication.

If we approach employee communication with a commitment to move the needle, and management can see a payoff in wiser benefit use, lower waste or higher productivity linked to our communication efforts, we'll find ourselves standing on firm ground and be able to show a substantial Return on Investment (ROI). But this won't happen until we can start measuring impact.

Step 7. Evaluate and Revise

As we noted above, we won't be able to defend our efforts until we can show that what we do works. This means that we must carefully evaluate where employees are through behavioral measurements before our communication efforts begin, so that we can target our communications to get them to where we want them to be. This means doing everything by the numbers.

The final step in this cybernetic, or *looped,* process is to evaluate what we did to see if it worked, and then to make any changes that we need to get it right. Once we have a baseline established, it is not difficult to go back and measure impact. Once we do, we have a ready blueprint for our next steps.

To sum it up, establishing a communication program involves having top management make a commitment, writing out a clear policy, assigning responsibilities, benchmarking, and then implementing, measuring and revising programs.

INVOLVING EMPLOYEES

Now that we've looked at a system for communication planning, it's time to appreciate the need for a comfortable, friendly environment that will be conducive to communication. We now move from *tech* to *touch*.

Managers have a responsibility to talk to their employees about the business. But exactly *what* should managers talk to employees about? Besides specific messages about business objectives, there are a number of basic questions and issues that need to be continuously addresed:

1. What is the mission of the unit?

Employees must know the organization's mission, vision and values, but they are usually more concerned with their own division rather than with the company in general.

► Summarize the corporate mission statement for an employee group:

____

____

____

____

____

____

► Write out your unit's specific mission:

____

____

____

____

____

____

INVOLVING EMPLOYEES (continued)

2. What are the employees' responsibilities?

Employees want to know what they will be judged on and what they are expected to do. Much of this can be accomplished during orientation on the first day of work when an employee is most impressionable.

List three responsibilities for one of your employees, that is, the key ones that he or she will be evaluated on:

- ______________________________
- ______________________________
- ______________________________

3. How are employees performing?

In more and more companies, compensation is being linked more to performance and less to seniority. Employee and employee teams need to get feedback on a frequent basis. *Annual* performance reviews are not enough to keep people motivated. Performance feedback should be continuous, even weekly, so that when the annual evaluation is made, there are no surprises. Continuous dialogue on performance can also help lead to successful employee development.

Identify opportunities during the coming month for communicating with one of your employees or employee teams regarding their performance:

Project	Milestone	Date to Communicate

4. **Address the individual needs and concerns of employees.**

Smart companies understand that personal problems can impact job performance, and, therefore, have developed employee assistance programs to help with problems such as *substance abuse, economic problems* and *family difficulties.* Supervisors must be trained to identify these problems and taught how to get help for employees when necessary.*

Exercise: Time for Counseling

John's performance has slipped in the last couple of weeks. He seems on edge and distracted. Write out some of the questions that you might ask him:

____

____

____

Remember that, in dealing with an employee who seems to have personal problems, your primary concern is job performance. Your questions should, therefore, relate to helping to improve the employee's performance. Personal problems are only an issue if they relate to performance, so remember to keep your focus on getting help so that the employee can return to full productivity.

5. **Get feedback.**

An employee's ideas and suggestions for improvement are important. In some companies this goes as far as sending employees across the country to deal directly with customers, or to look at videos of the product in use.

List three ways that you have used or might be able to use to get constructive feedback from your employees:

- ______________________________
- ______________________________
- ______________________________

*For more information on this subject, order *Coaching and Counseling,* by Marianne Minor. Menlo Park, CA: Crisp Publications, Inc., 1989.

INVOLVING EMPLOYEES (continued)

6. How does their unit compare with other units?

Employees are very interested in their own worksite and what is going on there. It's nice to get a publication once in a while informing them about how the corporation is doing, but it's more important to know how their unit stacks up against others in the company, against the competition and against their unit's own previous record.

What are the standards of comparisons for your unit? List two or three examples:

- ____
- ____
- ____

Are these being communicated to employees? ☐ YES ☐ NO

To be effective, there are some key messages that we must communicate to employees on a regular basis:

- ''This is our mission . . . and here is how you fit in.''
- ''What you do here is important.''
- ''Let me tell you how you are doing.''
- ''Let me help you do your job better.''
- ''Let me help you with your personal problems.''
- ''Here is how our unit did this quarter . . .''
- ''We've made a mistake, but here's how we are going to fix it.''
- ''What are your ideas?''

Starting Today . . .

Here are some suggestions for making immediate improvements in employee communication:

► *Increase contact and communication between management and the shop floor.*

The best way to go about this is to create opportunities—formally through increased meetings and feedback sessions, but also informally by getting out of the office. Staff visits to the shop floor and office areas build credibility, boost morale and show that management is visibly involved at the local level. Sound like a political campaign? It is.

Even more radical is the idea to ask the plant staff to take turns in the shop *working on various hourly jobs.* Other approaches include *Brown Bag Lunches* with employees to tell them what is going on and to answer any questions they may have. In larger organizations *Skip-Level Lunches,* in which top management meets with lower-level managers, help keep senior managers on their toes and give them an opportunity to see if communication really is going up and down the line.

Make a list of three new communication actions that you can take now:

- ____
- ____
- ____

► *Make supervisors and managers accountable for relaying information.*

Install systems that force managers to document their delivery of information to employees. Some companies institute a reverse evaluation system, in which employees rate their managers on a number of factors, including communication.

List some accountability tools that might work well in your organization:

- ____
- ____
- ____

INVOLVING EMPLOYEES (continued)

► *Develop channels that get information to supervisors and managers quickly.*

With today's high-speed telecommunications and information systems, getting information to all levels of management can be simple and efficient. Companies everywhere are utilizing computer E-mail and voice mail to quickly get information out to supervisors. In many instances just updating the bulletin board can make a big difference in improving communication.

What channels could you be using more effectively?

- ____
- ____
- ____

► *Tell employees how their unit is doing compared with other units and the company as a whole.*

This is the job that managers can do face-to-face. Most employees care more about this than they do about the four-color magazines about corporate events.

List three outputs that you can measure for your unit: *(For example, customer complaints, hours of overtime, etc.)*

- ____
- ____
- ____

► *Expand upward communications.*

There is no easy way to do this. Suggestion programs that provide both recognition and monetary rewards have produced annual savings of millions of dollars to companies that support the programs through aggressive communication. Other ideas include personal interviews, contests, mail surveys, water cooler chats and rap sessions during lunch or after hours. What might work for your unit?

- ____
- ____
- ____

HUMAN RESOURCE COMMUNICATION

Organizations today are making a number of strategic human resource changes: reducing benefits, restructuring and downsizing, putting more compensation at risk, linking rewards more closely to performance, and providing increased training and employee assistance. The trend is to reduce personnel costs as much as possible without losing the ability to attract and retain good employees.

To make the organization more competitive, management must get employees to buy into the company's mission, vision and values. This strategic role is new and often involves links between communication and human resources officials.

Communication Check-Up

Check ☑ which of the following you have received communications about in your organization in the last year:

- ☐ Mission, vision and values
- ☐ Changes in salary administration programs
- ☐ Training and development opportunities
- ☐ Employee assistance programs
- ☐ Benefits
- ☐ Diversity policy
- ☐ New retirement or separation options
- ☐ Americans with Disabilities Act provisions
- ☐ Charitable contributions
- ☐ New personnel policies and procedures
- ☐ National Labor Relations Act
- ☐ Equal Employment Opportunity
- ☐ OSHA

HUMAN RESOURCE COMMUNICATION (continued)

An organizational communication program strongly supports human resources programs. As a matter of fact, the linkage is so strong today that in as many as one third of all companies, the function of employee communication is located in Human Resources (HR).

Human resource managers need to help professional communicators to:

- Identify communication priorities
- Establish capabilities and assign responsibilities
- Develop and implement programs which are linked to organizational goals.

A human resource strategy for the *communications* department will include:

- Benchmarking employee concerns via an attitude survey
- Developing specific program activities along with HR
- Producing materials and executing programs
- Evaluating results for linkage to corporate objectives

Example: Communicating a Human Resource Program

A new substance abuse program has been developed at the corporate level, but the plant employee relations manager or the plant manager must communicate it, answer questions and make sure it is implemented. Companies are training managers at all levels of the organization to become more involved in the delivery of human resource services.

Exercise: Human Resource Communications

Describe how an HR program was communicated in your organization in the recent past:

► Name of the program: ______________________________________

____

► The program was communicated by: ____________________________

____

In an environment where employees want to hear information from their supervisors, internal communications people must produce materials that supervisors can use for a targeted work audience—production workers, office staff, managers and unionized labor.

But giving managers information to communicate to employees is only part of the process—those managers must understand how important this is to their job. Managers must be given training in interpersonal communication, and their financial reward must be at least partially based on how well they communicate with their employees in order to make the system work.

The development of appropriate HR communication materials must be a joint exercise between HR and communications that results in messages which are clearly matched to specific corporate HR objectives, delivered according to a specific timetable and evaluated in terms of measurable behavioral changes.

SPECIAL HUMAN RESOURCE COMMUNICATION ISSUES

Mergers

Companies involved in mergers will have significant communication problems, mostly because there is so much energy being focused on putting the deal together and executing the merger, that things like communicating to employees seem to get lost in the shuffle. Identifying communication as a major issue up front, and identifying responsible officials in both HR and communications to work as a team on the problem, will reduce some of the negative consequences.

Companies that are engaged in these activities say that the biggest problem they have is finding the time to communicate face-to-face and in staff meetings.

If there was a merger within your company in the last few years, describe the good and bad ways that communication was handled:

Good Ways: ______________________________

____

Bad Ways: ______________________________

____

Cutbacks

When companies cut back their work forces, most of the care and concern is directed toward those who are leaving. But what about those who remain? The job dissatisfaction level of survivors increases, there is decreased productivity, and performance goes down. Rumors can reach hurricane force. At this time, when everybody is hurting, communication can make an enormous contribution to getting things back to a state of normality. What should managers be doing?

Here is a short list:

- Establish a pipeline to get into the rumor loop.
- Confront rumors with facts.
- Move quickly to confirm or deny rumors.
- Make sure there is a way for employees to get information about rumors.

This is a time when survivors are going to be called on to work together and take up the slack. They need to be led and motivated.

Were there cutbacks at your company recently? From a communications point of view, what was done right and what was not? ______________________

____

Mistakes made during cutbacks: ______________________________

____

How well do you think his manager handled communicating the news of a cutback?

Pay Programs

Compensation strategies today are putting more and more emphasis on compensation at risk as an inducement to greater performance. For *salaried employees,* the move is to individual plans which link annual increases to achievement of measurable, written objectives. For *hourly or nonexempt employees,* new plans put a percentage of compensation paid based on team performance against established goals. Other new compensation models include lump sum or one-time payments, which are performance-based bonuses and not a part of base compensation.

With these pay philosophy changes, compensation communication is becoming more important than ever. Employees rank it as one of their key areas of information need. As companies move toward more performance-based systems, it is important that employees understand what the rules are and how they can compete for additional dollars.

This approach requires managers to become key interpreters of compensation plans, since it is those same managers who will be required in many cases to establish performance criteria.

Exercise: Communicating About Pay

Here is a typical series of objectives for communicating an employee pay program. Check ☑ those that are part of your organization's program:

- ☐ Provides a timely announcement of the new program or changes to those affected
- ☐ Answers immediate questions that participants may have
- ☐ Emphasizes fair and equitable administration of the salary program
- ☐ Gives managers and supervisors the knowledge and skills to implement the program
- ☐ Provides continuing communications during the development phase
- ☐ Demonstrates the relationship of pay, benefits and job environment as parts of total compensation
- ☐ Offers employees the opportunity to get feedback with questions, concerns, perceptions and attitudes concerning the organization's pay program

An effective salary program provides information on the following:

- Why a new program is being implemented, or why changes are being made
- The objectives of the new program
- How job evaluation is conducted
- How the program provides internal equity; fairness for all
- What is the company's pay philosophy: To pay at market rates? To be the top payer?
- The external competitiveness of the program.

Identify audience targets and needs as follows:

- Provide top management with sufficient information to gain commitment and support to make policy decisions. Get their top reports on evaluation committees.
- Salary administrators must be made knowledgeable of the details of the operation of the program.
- Supervisors require detailed information in order to be able to answer employee questions and make salary recommendations.
- Employees must be provided with an overview of the program; they need to know that their performance will be rewarded and that the program is fair and competitive.

Conduct research to find out:

- What employees already know
- What information they have received
- What misinformation they have received
- What their general feelings and perceptions are

SPECIAL HUMAN RESOURCE COMMUNICATION ISSUES (continued)

The media that you use to communicate this information depends on the demographic profile of your employees; for example, how many locations are involved, your organizational style, budget concerns and whether the communication will be reused during orientation. Possible media might include:

- Letters or memos, which are best for announcement of programs.
- Articles in employee publications, which are best for updates on the program's progress. Key points should include representation from all parts of the company that are involved in the process.
- Employee meetings utilizing audiovisual and question and answer sessions.

A visually-oriented program works best, such as a video or slides with a take-away brochure that graphically shows the entire process. The brochure should also feature a message from the CEO, a diagram of the pay evaluation program, and the most commonly asked questions and their answers. Other ways to communicate include highlight folders, payroll stuffers, telephone hotlines or tape message systems, posters and bulletin boards, and employee handbooks.

Make sure that your communication plan is linked to milestones, beginning with the start of the evaluation process and concluding with a major communication effort during roll-out. This period can run from six months to a year.

Compensation programs should not be communicated in a vacuum. Benefits are part of total compensation, so performance evaluations should be closely linked to compensation. These links must be communicated to all employees. The best way to communicate this information is through supervisors in their subject areas.

How was the compensation program in your organization communicated to you most recently? ______________________________

____

____

____

____

Benefits

Benefits communication can motivate employees to get more involved in choosing new options that match their needs and can save their organization money.

Benefits communication has become a priority today as:

- Companies install new flexible benefit programs that give employees the opportunity to get involved in designing individualized programs.
- Companies seek to provide more cost-effective benefits in the face of rising health care costs, often through new cost-sharing arrangements with employees.
- Government tax policy on benefits continues to change and legislation aimed at national health care reform is becoming more complex.
- As America ages, retirement planning is particularly complex because of new legislation, longer life spans and rising health care costs for covered retirees.

KEY ELEMENTS OF A BENEFITS COMMUNICATION PLAN

Studies show that employees do not read written benefits material that is not completely communicated. This can cost both the employee and the company money when bad choices are the result.

Eight-Step Method for Improvement

This step-by-step approach for developing a benefits communication plan includes:

STEP 1 Conduct Research

Should the communications be low-key or glitzy? High-tech interactive software or just a handout? The best way to find out is to ask employees through focus groups how they would like to get their information. If a company has been going through hard times, then it will make sense to be low-key. The reason for glitzy communications is that they get through to people.

STEP 2 Develop a Strategy

The most important step in the whole process of communication is determining the audience and the correct messages to relay. While all employees may be covered under the plan, a good communication strategy recognizes that there are a number of employee subgroups—new hires, mid-career people, those near retirement—with differing needs. Today, benefits are designed with the needs of these subgroups in mind, and the accompanying communications must address them.

Include a time-line for implementation. Budgets for communications can vary greatly, but a reasonable minimum is about $30–$50 per employee.

Benefits program changes, such as increasing health care contributions, should be explained in the wider context of what is happening in society as a whole. In summary, a program must not only inform, but also motivate employees to take action.

STEP 3 Hand out Materials

These can include descriptions, benefit statements, worksheets, and enrollment and beneficiary forms. They should be developed and presented to employees in a folder.

STEP 4 Schedule Presentations

Presentations are ideal for small groups and should be conducted whenever major changes are made. Small groups allow more opportunities for questions and answers. Larger groups are more time efficient, but can add to downtime costs and require supplemental question-and-answer materials or forms. For large and/or dispersed organizations, new technologies such as E-mail or voice mail can be used, but they remove the people factor.

STEP 5 Prepare Visually Based Communciations

These should be a part of all presentations. Employees today are video watchers. The problem with so many benefits videos and slide shows is that they look as though they were produced by a tax accountant.

Calculations and complex explanations should be saved for printed materials. The power of the visual medium is to use real-life examples to demonstrate concepts to people. Try to keep visual communications simple. Stick with highlights and use diagrams and easy-to-understand flow charts and graphics.

STEP 6 Prepare Coordinated Print Pieces

Handouts should accompany all visual presentations. A take-away print piece reminds employees of the highlights of the presentation.

STEP 7 Use Interactive Components

A number of interactive computer programs are now available. The overall goal is to address individual questions concerning complex programs.

STEP 8 Evaluate the Results

Evaluations will tell you if the program worked. Simple mail-back cards with questions designed to test the effectiveness of the communication effort will help ensure that the program is working.

KEY ELEMENTS OF A BENEFITS COMMUNICATION PLAN (continued)

Benefit communication tools to choose from include the following:

Standard Packages:
A number of insurance and benefits consulting firms have developed generic communications and enrollment packages that can be adapted for budget-minded companies.

Television:
Videos can be very good at delivering an impression, or a feeling, about programs. They also can serve to point out highlights and to deliver the company's message on correct benefit use. Many businesses use take-offs on popular television shows to get the point across. The MTV generation has come to expect a snappy look.

Interactive Computer Software:
Levi Strauss & Co. has one of the most advanced programs, OLIVER, the "On-Line Interactive Visual Employee Resource," where employees can tie in to the main frame and not only look at possible benefits, but also areas such as financial planning, training and development.

Automated Voice Response:
This technology allows users to enter their selections via voice mail after they have read over materials sent to them by mail.

Print:
Even if it is on a computer disk, you are still reading words. Print is the oldest and most basic communication tool for explaining benefits to employees. Today, print is seen as a supplement to more advanced communication technologies, but it works fine by itself in a pinch, especially with interactive pieces such as worksheets.

Meetings:
Most employees still prefer to get information on a one-on-one basis from supervisors. Small and large group meetings don't rank as high with employees unless strong graphic elements are present, such as a video or slide show.

Slides and Overheads:
This is the traditional method benefits information is presented in meetings. This is not very high-tech, but it allows the presenter to interject himself or herself into the presentation. In the past, however, too many of these shows have tended to look like accounting presentations.

Video Conferences:
These are evangelical in nature, bringing the corporate faithful together by satellite across the nation or around the world to hear about the new program and what it means for employees. This is a good but expensive technique for waving the flag on benefits.

Hotlines:
For medium- to large-sized organizations this is an important tool for employees to have access to for getting very specific answers to their questions. The problem is that hotlines need to be adequately staffed by knowledgeable specialists.

Payroll Processing Systems:
Information on benefits is directly communicated to employees via each payroll statement, so that an employee knows where he or she stands regarding benefits at all times. This will cut down many of the employee's questions.

Special communication activities can include:

- Enrollment marketing for benefits such as 401(k) programs and others which require a vote by employees before they can be instituted. Communication campaigns for this effort should follow all of the rules of marketing, emphasizing product, placement, promotion and pricing.

- Wellness communications on fitness, nutrition, managing stress and smoking can make a real difference. For small- and medium-sized companies, general publications and customized periodicals may be available and can be very useful.

Based on the descriptions on page 56, what would you do to improve your organization's benefits communication program? ______________________________

____

____

____

____

ENCOURAGING FEEDBACK

Getting employee feedback is the first step on the road to finding out how close we are to the real world. Employee feedback provides an even greater value when employees are not only willing to talk about themselves but are also willing to suggest ideas that may help to improve the organization's performance.

IBM's often-mentioned *Speak Up!* feedback program, for example, has resulted in 400,000 questions and concerns being voiced by employees in the 32 years since it first began.

In designing feedback systems, the question always comes up: Should an upward communication program be anonymous? The answer is very complex. In a traditional company, it is yes. In a more advanced, evolving organization, frank and candid comments from identifiable employees will be valued. The larger the organization, the more difficult it is to accomplish upward communication.

Exercise

Below is a list of feedback systems. Check ☑ the ones that are used in your organization. Highlight the ones that you would like to try:

1. Systems for listening via first-line supervisors:

- ☐ personal interviews
- ☐ face-to-face meetings with small groups
- ☐ an open door that is really open

2. Methods for employee publications:

- ☐ mail or telephone surveys
- ☐ monitor how many publications go directly to the wastebasket
- ☐ remove a regular feature of your publication and measure any complaints that follow
- ☐ do "man-on-the-street" interviews on specific topics, and publish them

3. Unit systems:

☐ informal suggestion programs

☐ search out 10 people in your unit, arm yourself with a set of questions, and go find the answers

4. Corporate systems:

☐ an employee council that meets regularly with top management

☐ encourage and print candid letters in employee publications

☐ evaluation forms for corporate communication programs

☐ a rumor hot-line, especially during difficult times

☐ manager appraisals conducted by employees

☐ publication readership surveys

☐ formal suggestion programs

☐ video viewership surveys

☐ formal attitude surveys

ENCOURAGING FEEDBACK (continued)

Providing incentives such as recognition or small monetary rewards for new ideas has long been recognized as an effective means of encouraging employee feedback.

As organizations begin to focus more on internal as well as external customer service, it is important for units to get feedback from the people that they service. For example, have the accounting department get feedback on the turnaround of travel vouchers, or the marketing department get feedback from engineering on the scheduling of deliveries.

Effective feedback will work in organizations where it is welcomed, rewarded, recognized and, most importantly, acted on.

Studies show that rewards do not have to be large, although in some organizations they can equal a percentage of the savings that an employee achieves. Most of the time, a token reward and high praise will work just as well. Recognition can be valued by workers as much as, and even more than, money.

Putting a picture of the employee with this month's ''Bright Idea'' in the company newsletter will go a long way toward communicating to everyone that ideas, suggestions and feedback are being rewarded. But the final reward to employees will come from knowing that their ideas will be implemented.

Negative Feedback

What about whistleblowing and negative feedback? Some organizations fall apart when a whistleblower points out wrongdoing, or an employee provides negative information that may be correct but will hurt some senior manager's ego. Thus, the credibility of feedback systems can quickly go out the door. Good systems usually go bad during difficult times, such as during cutbacks.

EVALUATING COMMUNICATION PROGRAMS

How do we know whether our communication program is working? Previously, we explained the importance of *benchmarking* employee commitment to the objectives established by the organization. In this way, we are able to measure the value of specific communication campaigns.

In this section, we will look at *how to measure the communication system itself.*

There are two types of measurements for employee communication: *attitude surveys* and *communication audits.* The attitude survey sometimes focuses on communication, but is also sometimes broader in scope, telling us what the climate and perception of employees are, and what can be done to improve them.

An *employee attitude survey* can measure a wide range of subjects, including job climate, security, satisfaction, opportunities for communication, management, compensation and benefits.

A *communication survey* measures:

- communication philosophy
- topics which are important to employees
- whether employees feel sufficiently informed
- employees' preferred sources of information
- the readership levels for publications
- communications' credibility and usefulness
- managers' communication skills
- awareness by employees of the company's mission, vision and values

EVALUATING COMMUNICATION PROGRAMS (continued)

Communication audits can model how the communication process is working in the organization, based on the stated goals, the resources committed and the perceptions of the employees. The audit can determine the credibility of management and the effectiveness of supervisory communications. Audits can measure employee attitudes and their knowledge of the company, the effectiveness of feedback programs, and the impact of corporate media.

Techniques used in communication audits may include:

- *Focus groups:* small groups of people representing the various demographics of employee groups. Focus groups provide qualitative information, which means that they show not only employees' opinions, but also the context of those opinions.

- *Management climate assessment:* generally a series of interviews with top management and key unit managers used to determine the culture and values of the organization in relation to communication. This can also be used to identify the effects of individual personalities and to define the content of jobs and roles.

- *Content evaluation of published material:* looks at the subject matter of memos, policies, forms, newsletters and the *paper* that a corporation uses to determine what is important based on what is written down and maintained.

- *Surveys:* provide a means to let everyone in the organization get involved in the audit process (see Appendix). Surveys allow people to participate anonymously. This data is more quantitative than qualitative.

- *Network analysis:* looks at the interaction among people in an organization to determine or map such things as communication nodes or bottlenecks. The theory is that the more people interact, the more successful an organization is.

An attitude survey or communication audit is normally used when there has been some major change in the organization, such as realignment, downsizing or reengineering.

WHICH IS BETTER: *QUANTITATIVE* OR *QUALITATIVE* RESEARCH?

As organizational communicators take their first steps toward improving communication, they have tended to lean toward qualitative over quantitative research. The most popular qualitative techniques include *interviews* and *focus groups.* Focus groups of 6–12 people can be organized and conducted relatively quickly. Over a one- to three-hour period you can identify an audience, test a message and confirm the direction you are going. Focus groups are also relatively inexpensive.

Researchers generally tend to look down at this technique unless it is tied to an actual survey because it lacks the scientific validity that formal survey research provides.

Another qualitative technique, the *in-depth interview,* provides an open-ended interview in which the interviewee is given a subject and then encouraged to expand on it in his or her own terms. This type of research can be valuable early on in the process to evaluate the kind of climate or environment in which the research will be conducted.

The key quantitative research tool is the *survey.* Questionnaires are generally more expensive to develop, test and administer. They can range from the more elaborate face-to-face interview, to a short telephone interview. Questionnaires can be passed out at the office or at the plant for employees to fill out, or they can be mailed so that they can be done at home. The design and administration of questionnaires should be conducted by professional researchers, usually outside contractors, who will often use a focus group to design questions.

COMMUNICATION RESEARCH AND CHANGE

One of the real problems with research is that sometimes it tells you what you don't want to hear—that management is hopelessly out of touch with its employees, that middle managers don't care about communicating to employees and that nobody believes in the company newsletter.

People who stand to lose the most have a direct interest in trying to discredit the research. It is, therefore, important to set up processes for getting past this problem:

- ► Provide feedback that makes sense.
- ► Get commitment to take action before doing the research.
- ► Relate actions to research; tell people that their input helped.
- ► Measure how actions worked; find out if what you did worked.

The level of reaction to research can range from full implementation to full rejection, with the worst outcome probably being a decision to do nothing.

Communication research is most helpful in choosing among possible alternatives while designing communications, and then making changes in the organization to respond to that feedback.

Measuring the impact of communication programs becomes more important than ever if we expect to convince top management that it pays, middle managers that it works, and everyone that it has true value.

SECTION

III

Your New Communication Toolkit

THE IMPACT OF NEW TECHNOLOGY

> *"We are in great haste to construct a magnetic telegraph from Maine to Texas; but Maine and Texas, it may be, have nothing important to communicate."*
>
> —Henry David Thoreau

What tools do I use to communicate with? The simple answer is, the ones that will do the job.

New communication technologies have increased the speed of communication, the amount of information that can be sent, and the accessibility of it to a wider group of people inside and outside of the organization.

Some years back the author visited a new million-dollar video training facility that had been assembled by a utility company. It seemed to be a wonderful idea, until it was explained that the facility was rarely used because of staff cuts. The moral: You can have the best communication tools possible, but they are worthless unless properly used.

The impact of the new communication technologies has also greatly changed the ways that we acquire information. We are changing from a society of *readers* to one of *viewers.* For example, readership of newspapers in the United States has remained steady at about 60 million for the past 25 years, even though the population has continued to grow. Studies are showing that most people under 25 do not get their information from print media; rather they get it from radio and television.

There are some major differences between print and visual media, as this chart shows:

Print Medium	Video Medium
Intelligence	Emotions
Detailed	Brief
Abstract	Concrete
Nonlinear	Serial
Big Picture	Specifics
Enduring	Ephemeral
Issues	Stories
Complex	Simple

YOUR NEW COMMUNICATION TOOLKIT (continued)

Studies by professional communicators have shown for years that most employees want to get information about their companies primarily from their supervisors, and that choices of other media rank lower.

Below is a list of preferred channels of communication according to a 1990 study. Re-rank these media in terms of how information is actually delivered in your organization.

Current vs. Preferred Sources of Information

	Current Source (%)	Preferred Source (%)	My Ranking
Top executives	15	62	_______
Small group meetings	37	70	_______
Immediate supervisor	59	90	_______
Orientation program	22	45	_______
Local employee publication	18	41	_______
Large group meetings	28	49	_______
Annual business report to employees	17	37	_______
Audiovisuals	13	29	_______
Upward communication programs	14	29	_______
Employee handbook	33	46	_______
Company-wide employee publication	29	36	_______
Bulletin boards	38	38	_______
Mass media	15	12	_______
The grapevine	42	9	_______

Source: *Towers Perrin* 1990. Reprinted with permission.

Below is a description of media and their relative strengths and weaknesses. As you read through them, check those that are being used in your organization. Circle those which you feel might hold promise:

Meetings

Meeting with employees, individually or as a group, is the classic employee communication tool. In most organizations that are well-run, there is continuous interaction among people throughout the day. Managers and supervisors complain of endless hours spent in meetings. The kind of meetings that tend to be more productive are the ones on-the-fly—a quick chat with production workers or customer service representatives, a chance meeting with a counterpart in another department, or a cup of coffee with the accounts receivable director, whose department has a bottleneck.

Hard-working managers have often assumed too much work and can not find the time to communicate with their people. Better managers have lots of time for communication because they are keeping tabs on those people who actually do the work, to make sure they are on schedule and to get their feedback on improving the process and product.

MEETING STYLES	PROS	CONS
Individual Meetings with Supervisor	Personal	Time Consuming
Small Group Meetings with Supervisor	Team Building	Time Consuming
Unit Meetings	All Get on the Same Wavelength	Lost Productivity
Large Group Sessions and Briefings	Single Message for All	Lost Productivity
Skip-Level Management Meetings	Good feedback	Infrequent

YOUR NEW COMMUNICATION TOOLKIT (continued)

Print Media

A memo from the boss, a newsletter, a pamphlet on benefits, the bulletin board—classic print media are the old standbys of organizational communication. In the communication chain these are usually corporate office media, although this is changing in today's flattened out organizational structure. Daily or weekly one-page tip sheets duplicated on the copier are providing quicker dissemination of news at the unit level. Employee annual reports that speak of employee and organizational accomplishments are becoming more popular. Employee magazines seem to be most effective when they are mailed home. This also helps to keep the family in touch with organizational developments.

PRINT MEDIA	PROS	CONS
Daily or Weekly Tip Sheets	Current Information	Rarely Done
Bulletin Boards	Latest Information	Must Be Updated Constantly
Pamphlets	Good for Human Resources	Not Easy to Find
Payroll Inserts	Good Channel	Single Message Each Time
Letters and Memos	Direct to Employee	Can Get Lost in the Clutter
Monthly Newsletters	Old Standby	Often Not Credible or Focused on Business Issues
Employee Magazines	Slick	Should Be Sent Home
Employee Annual Reports	Becoming Popular	Need Balance Between Employee and Organization

Feedback Channels

The wave of our media future may be interactivity—feeding back through our television sets, computers and telephones. The feedback potential for organizational communication hasn't even begun to be explored. Some corporations are setting up E-mail bulletin boards so that employees can trade suggestions and ideas up, down and sideways in the organization. Hotlines with a real voice on the other end are a good way to encourage feedback and to rebut the grapevine.

"Secret Shopper" is a post office program in which a "mystery" employee monitors information flow. When information is received by him or her, this employee drops the communication manager a note or gives a call to let him or her know what message has been delivered.

FEEDBACK	PROS	CONS
Suggestion Programs	Can Create Millions in Savings	Must be Credible
Hotlines	Fast	Must Be Manned
Fax-backs	Easy to Use	Must Be Responded To

YOUR NEW COMMUNICATION TOOLKIT (continued)

Electronic Systems

In the spread-out, flattened-out, loosely structured organization of the future, electronic channels offer the best hope for communication.

E-mail can provide every linked employee with a daily electronic newsletter featuring the organization's morning news, its weekly calendar, a roundup of news coverage, management memos and so on.

Voice messaging brings us the voice of top managers. Voice messaging can mimic many of the characteristics of E-mail, providing daily news updates and targeted information for specific groups, like managers and field sites.

Video was very popular in the 1980s until companies realized that videos can be expensive to produce and may even end up not being watched. But the lure of video still remains. Why? Because the American public watches television five to seven hours a day. Television provides a consistent message, can be viewed at will, and can have strong mental and sensory impacts.

Teleconferences, linking different sites together, have proved their worth for organizations, at the same time saving on air fare. Live satellite videoconferences connecting the organization together in a one-way video, two-way audio environment have often been used for major announcements and product roll-outs.

Broadcasts using a public address system can be used in large work areas where employees are doing manual work. Announcements might take the form of a senior management statement or even a mini-newscast.

Newslines are telephone information lines updated daily/weekly with organizational news that can be accessed, usually via an 800-number, by employees at any time.

ELECTRONIC SYSTEMS	PROS	CONS
E-Mail	Fast Management Channel	All Must Have Access
Electronic Bulletin Boards	Good Lateral Communication	Can Become Cluttered
Voice Messaging	Excellent for Top Management to Speak to All Employees at Once; Immediate	Can Be Overused
Video Newsletter	Popular Medium	Takes Time Away from Work; Overused
Radio	Can Get to Employees and Community	Not Much Control
Audio Cassettes	Excellent for Sales or Scattered Work Force	Not for Big Groups
Live Satellite Hook-ups	Good for Scattered Organizations	Lots of Time and Money
Videotext/Internal Television	Accessible to All	Can Be Distracting

YOUR NEW COMMUNICATION TOOLKIT (continued)

Targeted Communications

An *Employee Information Center* is simply an area designated exclusively for communication activities, including videos, newsletters, even media releases, news clippings and accessible data bases.

Special back-channels on the organizational communication network are used to target information to special constituencies like management, headquarters staff, sales personnel, retirees and others. Most have been in print up to now. Desktop publishing technologies make producing these media easier, faster and less expensive. But don't ever mention the words *fast* or *cheap* in the same breath as the words *annual report.*

TARGET GROUPS	PROS	CONS
Management Newsletters	Keeps Managers Informed	Extra Reading
Headquarters Publications	Big Picture	Many Don't Care
Unit Publications	Focused	Too Busy
Sales Force Communications	Audio Cassettes Are Best	
Retiree Publications	Powerful Constituency	Expensive
Annual Report	Boosts Stock	Puffery

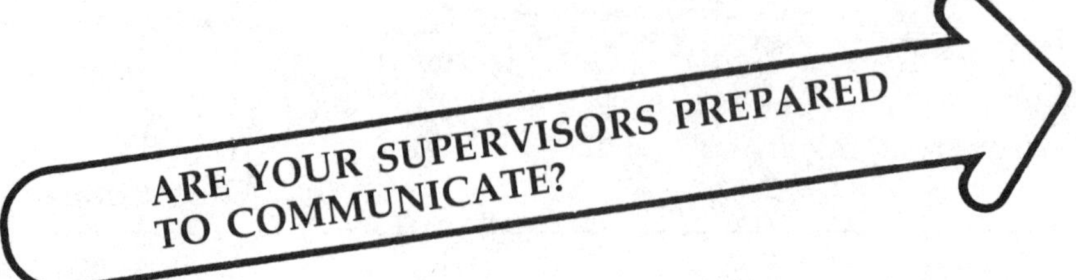

GETTING THE WORD OUT

Preparing Supervisors to Communicate

Lower-level managers have a lot of things on their minds: lots of work to do and many people to deal with. Communicating about events happening at corporate headquarters is not their main priority.

Supervisors and mangers often need to be encouraged to communicate. The only effective technique is *to make communication a major accountability in performance measurement and to link accomplishments to salary increases, incentives and promotions.* The term is a familiar one: *pay for performance.*

Today messages are too often:

Distorted
Misunderstood
Resisted
Neglected
Lost

Here are some reasons:

- CEOs and managers don't understand their responsibilities in communicating.
- A communication strategy that is ongoing and an action plan that is in place are missing.
- Executives never get beyond communicating WHAT, to WHY, to WHOM, WHEN, WHO by, or HOW.
- Organizations fail worst in communication at the times when communication is needed most—during cutbacks or bad times.
- Responsibility for communication is unclear, and communication efforts go unrewarded.

The results are mixed messages to employees and a lack of linkage of communication to the business.

GETTTING THE WORD OUT (continued)

Once the policy for communication has been established, and all of the programs and systems are in place, the next job is helping managers and supervisors to communicate.

EFFECTIVE MANAGERS:

- ✔ Provide positive and negative feedback
- ✔ Are experts in employee communication techniques
- ✔ Balance company/employee needs
- ✔ Challenge people to do their best
- ✔ Demonstrate a capacity for exercising control

Additional abilities that will aid people in being both good managers and communicators include: listening skills, team building, conflict resolution, and presentation and counseling skills.

For many supervisors, leading employees is not instinctive. Those who come up the ranks are usually appointed based on their proven job skills, not on their supervisory ability. Those who come from MBA programs usually have received no training in this area. *Supervisors must receive adequate training* to do their jobs effectively. In the leadership model, supervisors must also learn to become cheerleaders who help work teams accomplish their assignments. It is estimated that as much as 70 percent of a supervisor's time is spent in verbal communication, including active listening, and giving and receiving feedback.

Supervisors' jobs become particularly difficult when companies are downsizing and restructuring, and when reliable information is at a premium for everyone. When times are tough, some bosses resort to a rigid, controlling management style because they are threatened by more open systems. However, companies facing cutbacks should naturally drift toward a more open style because that is what allows them to take the greatest advantage of workers' skills. It is the only way for them to get by with fewer workers, not necessarily because they think it is the right way to conduct business.

TRAINING SUPERVISORS AND MANAGERS TO COMMUNICATE MUST BE A TOP PRIORITY

A ONE-TO-ONE FUTURE FOR EMPLOYEE COMMUNICATION?

In *The One-to-One Future,* an exceptionally forward looking book, Don Peppers and Martha Rogers (New York: Doubleday Currency Books, 1993) have painted an exciting picture of the future of marketing, where computer databases can combine with relationship building in defining a new way to think about selling through increasing the share of business per customer. This is a very powerful idea, and may have some important ramifications for the world of employee communication.

We already have extensive data on our employees in the human resources department. More is there for the asking. The question is, how can we "market" our organization to our employees in a way that delivers a greater "share" of their efforts?

In this book we have talked extensively about moving employees from being informed to taking action to achieve business objectives.

And many organizations already have taken some steps to building better employee relationships—through suggestion and recognition programs, through decentralized structures and empowerment.

The question for the future is: Can we develop a one-to-one relationship with each of our employees that motivates them to greater productivity in a time when the relationship between the employer and employees has sunk to such a low depth?

All the tools are in place. The motivation is there. What is lacking may be the ideas:

✔ Can we accurately identify the real stars, the real contributors, the ones who do the most for the organization, no matter what level?

✔ Do we have special communication channels for them to use so they can get through the layers quickly?

✔ Do we treat our stars the way we treat our best customers?

✔ Do we use our stars as role models and tell their success stories to other employees in the organization?

One-to-one employee communication may be limited only by our imagination. The potential for micro-communicating needs to be explored as our organizations and society become more connected but less in-touch.

APPENDIX

Employee Communication Survey

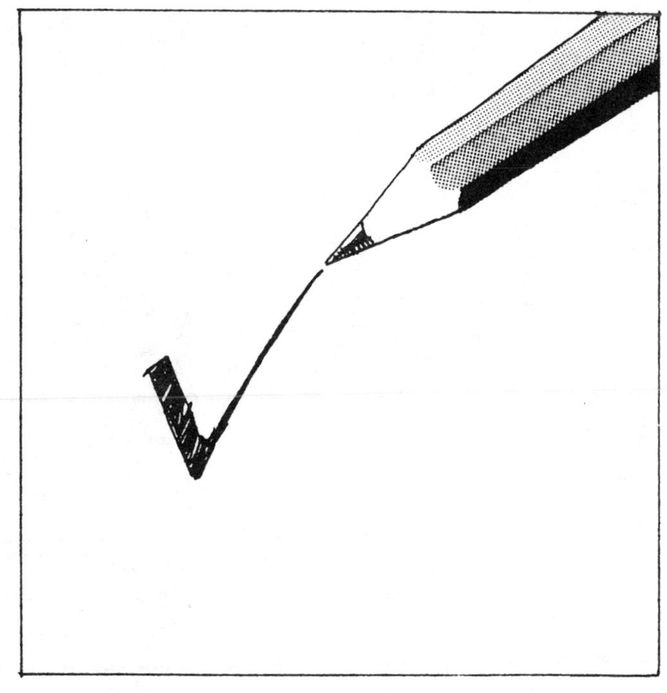

EMPLOYEE COMMUNICATION SURVEY

If an employee attitude survey has been conducted, it contains some general questions on communication that will be helpful. A communication survey like the one below will give you much more specific information.

This is an example of an employee communication survey. Check ''yes'' or ''no'' for the answers that are appropriate to conditions in your organization.

Communication Policy

	Yes	No
1. Is there a written communication policy in your organization?	☐	☐
2. Does the policy provide for two-way communication?	☐	☐
3. Does the policy have the active support of management?	☐	☐
4. Does the policy commit the organization to honesty and frankness?	☐	☐
5. Are communication objectives stated clearly?	☐	☐
6. Does one individual have overall responsibility for administering the policy?	☐	☐

Program

	Yes	No
1. Are there written procedures to implement the policy?	☐	☐
2. Do all communication activities and media conform to the policy, and are they coordinated?	☐	☐
3. Are the policy and programs regularly reviewed for effectiveness and compatibility?	☐	☐
4. Does top management take an active part in the program?	☐	☐

EMPLOYEE COMMUNICATION SURVEY (continued)

Delegated Authority

	Yes	No
1. Is there an organizational chart that shows communication channels?	☐	☐
2. Is accountability for communication defined?	☐	☐
3. Do supervisors know their accountabilities for relaying information up and down the line?	☐	☐

Keeping Supervisors Informed

	Yes	No
1. Are supervisors given advance information about the organization's plans and progress?	☐	☐
2. Are supervisors given the *why* of all matters transmitted directly through them to employees, so that they can discuss the subjects intelligently and answer any questions that may arise?	☐	☐
3. Is there a specific method for keeping top management regularly informed about employee thinking and rumors?	☐	☐
4. Do supervisors meet regularly with employees for discussions?	☐	☐
5. Is there a clear understanding between HR, communications, training and the supervisor as to what new employees are told and who is responsible for telling them?	☐	☐
6. Is there a checklist of items that should be covered with new employees?	☐	☐
7. Are employees encouraged to seek information from their supervisors?	☐	☐
8. Are supervisors trained to transmit information to employees and to answer their questions?	☐	☐

	Yes	No
9. Are bulletins given to supervisors before they are placed on bulletin boards?	☐	☐
10. Are there regular management meetings?	☐	☐
11. Do supervisors meet with each of their subordinates on a regular basis?	☐	☐
12. Is there a procedure for getting supervisors' ideas on labor contract improvements?	☐	☐
13. Is there a supervisor's manual for ready reference on all important problems?	☐	☐
14. Is there a manual of policies and procedures which is kept up-to-date, and is available to all supervisors?	☐	☐

Human Relations Communications

	Yes	No
1. Is HR's accountability for communication clearly defined?	☐	☐
2. Are communication duties clearly defined within HR?	☐	☐
3. Does HR operate with communications personnel in a way that facilitates communication through the system?	☐	☐
4. Does HR keep top management informed about potential *bombs* that might go off in personnel and labor matters?	☐	☐
5. Are the HR director and communication director involved in making top policy decisions?	☐	☐

EMPLOYEE COMMUNICATION SURVEY (continued)

Focus on Employee Interests

	Yes	No
1. Are employees' basic wants and interests (security, recognition, fair wages and opportunities to advance) considered in determining what information to present to the organization?	☐	☐
2. Are employees being given information about:		
—salary and benefits	☐	☐
—opportunities for advancement	☐	☐
—training opportunities?	☐	☐

Information About the Business

	Yes	No
1. Are employees given information about:		
—the background and philosophy of the organization	☐	☐
—the organization's products, services and customers	☐	☐
—how individuals can advance in the organization?	☐	☐
2. Are production plans and schedules shared?	☐	☐
3. Do employees know the employment plans for the months ahead?	☐	☐
4. Are public announcements reported to employees before being released to the external media?	☐	☐
5. Is the standing of the business in its industry made known to employees?	☐	☐

	Yes	No
6. Are employees told about:		
—the organization's goals and objectives	☐	☐
—building plans	☐	☐
—new products or services in advance	☐	☐
—research projects and developments	☐	☐
—important customers	☐	☐
—product or service successes	☐	☐
—advertising campaigns in advance	☐	☐
7. Do employees hear frequently about:		
—operating problems	☐	☐
—material shortages, if any	☐	☐
—customer complaints	☐	☐
—the "break-even" point	☐	☐
—the sales outlook	☐	☐
—the costs of doing business	☐	☐
—the need for greater productivity	☐	☐
—the organization's financial situation	☐	☐
—the organization's competitive position	☐	☐
—the impact of government regulation	☐	☐

EMPLOYEE COMMUNICATION SURVEY (continued)

	Yes	No
8. Do employees understand:		
—the organization's philosophy of employee relations	☐	☐
—financial issues facing the organization	☐	☐
—the value of their individual jobs?	☐	☐

Information About Employer-Employee Relations

	Yes	No
1. Does the company *sell* itself to its employees?	☐	☐
2. Does the top officer of the organization:		
—talk with employees in a group	☐	☐
—meet socially with employees	☐	☐
—visit informally with employees at their work stations?	☐	☐
3. Are new laws and regulations that affect employees explained to them?	☐	☐

General Business Conditions

	Yes	No
1. Are broad economic issues that affect the organization explained to employees?	☐	☐
2. Are employees informed about the company's position on government legislation and policy?	☐	☐

REVIEW

How do you interpret the data that you get from surveys?

What do the answers you get in surveys mean? Do you take the answers at face value, or do you weight them against national norms for your industry, climate and size? For example, you may find that only 43 percent of your managers feel that they get enough information to do their jobs effectively. While this number may raise some concerns for an individual organization, the number may be *average* for your industry and size. Some would conclude there is nothing to worry about. Others would say that you should only evaluate the data in the context of their organization. This is our feeling also . . . ***national norms are irrelevant.*** The real issue is whether there is something wrong that needs to be fixed. The answers can be found in the important numbers: profitability, a return-on-investment analysis and so on.

NOTES

NOTES

NOTES

NOTES

NOTES

NOTES

CRISP WORLDWIDE DISTRIBUTION

English language books are distributed worldwide. Major international distributors include:

ASIA/PACIFIC

Australia/New Zealand: In Learning, PO Box 1051, Springwood QLD, Brisbane, Australia 4127 Tel: 61-7-3-841-2286, Facsimile: 61-7-3-841-1580
ATTN: Messrs. Gordon

Singapore: 85, Genting Lane, Guan Hua Warehouse Bldng #05-01, Singapore 349569 Tel: 65-749-3389, Facsimile: 65-749-1129
ATTN: Evelyn Lee

Japan: Phoenix Associates Co., LTD., Mizuho Bldng. 3-F, 2-12-2, Kami Osaki, Shinagawa-Ku, Tokyo 141 Tel: 81-33-443-7231, Facsimile: 81-33-443-7640
ATTN: Mr. Peter Owans

CANADA

Reid Publishing, Ltd., Box 69559-109 Thomas Street, Oakville, Ontario Canada L6J 7R4. Tel: (905) 842-4428, Facsimile: (905) 842-9327
ATTN: Mr. Stanley Reid

Trade Book Stores: *Raincoast Books,* 8680 Cambie Street, Vancouver, B.C., V6P 6M9 Tel: (604) 323-7100, Facsimile: (604) 323-2600
ATTN: Order Desk

EUROPEAN UNION

England: *Flex Training,* Ltd. 9-15 Hitchin Street, Baldock, Hertfordshire, SG7 6A, England Tel: 44-1-46-289-6000, Facsimile: 44-1-46-289-2417
ATTN: Mr. David Willetts

INDIA

Multi-Media HRD, Pvt., Ltd., National House, Tulloch Road, Appolo Bunder, Bombay, India 400-039 Tel: 91-22-204-2281, Facsimile: 91-22-283-6478
ATTN: Messrs. Aggarwal

SOUTH AMERICA

Mexico: *Grupo Editorial Iberoamerica,* Nebraska 199, Col. Napoles, 03810 Mexico, D.F. Tel: 525-523-0994, Facsimile: 525-543-1173
ATTN: Señor Nicholas Grepe

SOUTH AFRICA

Alternative Books, Unit A3 Micro Industrial Park, Hammer Avenue, Stridom Park, Randburg, 2194 South Africa Tel: 27-11-792-7730, Facsimile: 27-11-792-7787
ATTN: Mr. Vernon de Haas